Directing Your First Movie !

John R. Collins

Directing Your First Movie !

A Beginner's Guide to
Making Movies with your Camera or Smartphone

Directing Your First Movie ! A Beginner's Guide to making Movies with your Camera or Smartphone

© John R. Collins
Edition : BoD - Books on Demand
12/14 rond-point des Champs Elysées
75008 Paris
Print by BoD Books on Demand, Norderstedt
ISBN : 9782322113040
Legal Deposit : September, 2016

"Whether in success or in failure, I'm proud of every single movie I've directed."

– Steven Spielberg

CONTENTS

INTRODUCTION	**9**
1 PRE-PRODUCTION	**11**
EXAMINING YOUR GOALS !	**12**
THE RIGHT SCRIPT	**14**
WRITING IT YOURSELF	*14*
OPTIONING A SCRIPT	*16*
STORYBOARDS	**17**
ESSENTIAL STORYBOARD ELEMENTS	*17*
ASSEMBLING THE CAST, CREW AND LOCATIONS	**18**
FINDING COMPETENT PROFESSIONALS TO ASSIST	*19*
WHEN AMATEURS WILL DO	*20*
CASTING ACTORS	*20*
LOCATION SCOUTING	*21*
2 FILM-MAKING STEP BY STEP	**22**
MONEY WELL SPENT	**22**
CAMERA AND SMARTPHONE	*22*
SOUND CAPTURE	*23*
MAKE-UP	*25*
CATERING AND CRAFT SERVICES	*26*
LIGHTING PACKAGES	*27*
BELIEVABLE SETS	*28*
ITEMS TO WORK AROUND	**29**
SPONSORSHIP DEALS	**30**
AVOIDING LEGAL AND LABOR PROBLEMS	**31**
USING TONE TO MAKE DIFFICULT SCRIPTS WORK	**32**
3 PRODUCTION	**33**
FILM OR DIGITAL?	**33**
MANAGING PRODUCTION TIME WISELY	**34**
STICKING TO A PRODUCTION SCHEDULE	*34*
THE IMPORTANCE OF PUNCTUALITY	*35*
KEEPING THE CREW BUSY AND HAPPY	**36**
LETTING YOUR CREW MANAGE THINGS	*36*
DIRECTOR OF PHOTOGRAPHY / CINEMATOGRAPHER	**37**
FIRST ASSISTANT DIRECTOR	**37**

LINE PRODUCER/PRODUCTION COORDINATOR	**38**
SCRIPT SUPERVISOR	**39**
YOUR ROLE AS DIRECTOR	**40**
DIRECTING ACTORS	*41*
GETTING THE COVERAGE YOU NEED	*42*
MONITORING TAKES	*42*
WHEN TO CALL IT A WRAP	*43*
4 POST-PRODUCTION	**45**
VIDEO	**45**
USING YOUR HOME COMPUTER	
OR A GOOD POST HOUSE?	*46*
FINAL EDIT	*47*
COLOR CORRECTION	*48*
AUDIO	**49**
ADDITIONAL DIALOG RECORDING (ADR)	*49*
FOLEY	*50*
OUTPUT AND DISTRIBUTION	**50**
CONCLUSION	**55**

INTRODUCTION

Directing your first movie ?– Sure, plenty of people go broke putting together a film that ends up looking as amateurish as you feel. This doesn't have to happen. Learn how to spend as little money as possible and put together your directorial début with funding and support from industry professionals. This notoriously difficult to penetrate career choice doesn't have to be impossible. Follow these rules and steps to success to make a reel film that doesn't suck. If you've watched, studied and loved film for years, perhaps you would make a good director. It's easy to get the bug, but how to actually make it happen? The ability to see a story in pictures and manage people is a must, but so is the ability to see the project through from one end to the other. There's hard work and long hours ahead, but if your goal is to have a finished project you can be proud to show around, you can do it, just as so many before you have. It's important to realize that just because it's not easy, doesn't mean that it can't be a fun and truly rewarding experience that you'll either talk about for years to come or actually set you off on a new career.

This book will show you how to go from your unrealized dream of being a director. We'll start of by showing you how to doing all the planning that will help this film project go off without a hitch and avoid some of the more common pitfalls that commonly plague first-time directors. Next, you'll get a look at the production itself, from how to keep your crew happy and productive to directing actors into giving the performance you've imagined. Lastly, your vision will truly come alive in the post-production process – this book will give you hints and tips for making the most of the footage you have.

More importantly, perhaps, this book will show you how to actually make enough money or notoriety that will allow you to make a second film, preferably with someone else's money.

1 - PRE-PRODUCTION

You may be surprised how much planning is *absolutely necessary* to guarantee the success of your directorial debut. It has been proven time and time again that there's nothing quite like skimping on this process to ensure chaos. If you're going to beat the odds, planning for contingencies and making sure you've got a road-map to will guide you through the entire process is essential. Don't kid yourself – making a movie is a *very* expensive proposition. Regardless of how you go about it, you will have to be extremely careful about how you spend your finite resources. Every moment you spend in production costs money, whether the camera is on or not. You can reasonably expect to spend 6-8 hours in pre-production for every hour in production.

EXAMINING YOUR GOALS !

Just what are you planning on doing with this film, anyhow? If your goal is to spend a weekend running around in the backyard with your pals and a camcorder, that's great. The pressure will be off and you can concentrate on having a good time. While you'll go through all the same basic steps, there will be less urgency and panic. Though the finished product won't likely look quite like what you've been seeing in your mind's eye, that's okay. As long as you don't go broke doing it – no harm, no foul. If you can't expect to get money out, you'll at least be aware that cash is only flowing one way and can plan accordingly. On the other hand, if you want to put together a short or feature-length film to bring around to festivals, that's quite another thing. This route is the classic long shot, but is also a chance for you to jump right in with both feet. This is most especially true in the case of short films of under 30 minutes. There are many festivals that specialize in such films, and this is a good way to impress potential investors with your skills and build notoriety. Should you be considering a feature, you should be aware that most successful film-makers recommend against this. It's just a lot to fund or bite into, as a time director. Funding concerns usually keep this from happening. If they don't, you've either found a sugar daddy or are doing things even more cheaply than is advisable. Of course, there are stories of folks who've gone against all such advice and made a name (and new directorial career) for themselves, but be advised, they are few and far between. It's often best to start small, even if you plan on ending up in the big time.

Another "middle road" type of film project is to put together a trailer for a feature-length film. This will serve as a portfolio piece that you can "shop" around and hopefully attract investment in the longer piece. Such a trailer, usually between 3-4 minutes, will prove beyond the shadow of a doubt that you know how to tell a visual story, bring a good crew together and create something that embodies all the elements of the feature-length film you hope to create with someone else's money.

In the end, you need to ask yourself if you're looking to actually make money from your first film or if you're willing to use this as an expensive crash course in film-making. Much of this book will focus on money-making prospects, though most of the concepts presented will apply, regardless.

THE RIGHT SCRIPT

Whether you write it yourself, hire someone to write something for you or find the very thing has landed right in your lap, you'll need a script (or at least a well-fleshed out idea) to begin the process. There are plenty of books available that outline the entire process, but there are a few basic ideas to keep in mind when deciding how to go about getting the script you need.

WRITING IT YOURSELF

Though there certainly are exceptions to this rule, it is considered good operating practice to refrain from writing the script yourself. There is such a thing as being "too close" to a project, and this is an easy way to do it. Many people consider the film-making process to be the essence of reinterpretation between words and images. If both parts of the process are yours, this can become confused, and that confusion will appear on screen. Be careful not to fall in love with your own words. It's far easier to pick dialog (and discard the rest) when it's written by someone else and there's no personal investment. A beautiful line is of no use to you if it doesn't move the story forward. Screen writing is, to some extent, minimalist, so you can expect to make some significant cuts from what you've written in the process of getting it down to a shootable script. If you do choose to do the writing yourself, you will at least have the advantage of being able to pen it according to your strengths. For instance, if you live somewhere with lots of space to shoot near ship-yards, you can set your tale near a wharf – that wouldn't work nearly as well in a land-locked area. You can also make allowances and plot twists that you'll be able to work around without spending extra money. In short, you can start with the ideal script. One way that many directors choose to start is to make a series of note cards that generally block out scenes and ideas. There's no need to actually put down dialog in such cards unless you have a good idea as to a key catchphrase you want to use. Otherwise, these will serve as your road-map to be knit together later, either by going directly to a script or to storyboards from which the actual script will be crafted from.

HIRING A WRITER TO SCRIPT YOUR IDEA

Perhaps more often, you'll need a "words person" to take your really great ideas and put them into something that resembles a usable script. Even if your plot outline is fairly well-formed, stiff and unbelievable dialog and gaping plot holes will most certainly be a problem. This is where a professional comes in. Even if he or she doesn't have a great deal of scriptwriting experience, getting a writer to put a bit of polish on a script will certainly help you to sell your final product.

Since film is inherently a collaborative effort, the scriptwriter you choose will have to be someone who actually can see your vision may be better at putting together. If the relationship turns adversarial for any reason, you may need to simply call the deal off, give them their work back, and start over. It never hurts to have a contract that spells out the rights and responsibilities of each party in case of success or failure. Though it may seem a bit heavy-handed, it's when people don't' have contracts that things can turn ugly.

OPTIONING A SCRIPT

Another option is to purchase someone else's existing script. As a first-time film-maker, you will be limited in what you're able to offer someone for their script. Given that most scripts take months and several re-writes to put together, it is very reasonable for a screenwriter to expect to be paid accordingly. That alone makes buying a script a somewhat less attractive option for a first-time director. There are, of course, ways around this. If possible, you'll want to see if you can offer a screenwriter a percentage of future profits rather than money up front. Sometimes you'll find new screenwriters who are so eager to have their work turned into a film they can show around and reference to in a resume, that you can get such scripts for a song. Though you'll limit yourself to young and "hungry" writers this way, if you're very picky about the script you use, this can work out quite well. Remember, screenplays are sold – not leased. You are able to change anything you like without consulting the author, so don't let yourself be bullied into accepting any part of a script you don't think works in your film. Often times, such a script will contain a great idea that you can then finesse into something usable yourself or with the help of another writer.

STORYBOARDS

The best way to get people to really see your vision is to commit it to paper. If you're a reasonably talented artist, you can do this yourself. Otherwise, don't be afraid to spend a few coins to pay someone else to do it. They certainly don't have to be works of art, but they must portray a preliminary vision of the film as you want to see it shot.

ESSENTIAL STORYBOARD ELEMENTS

When you're putting storyboards together, you want to make sure you get at least one frame for each different shot within each scene. Some scenes might have one or two frames and some might have 20. It should give you the visual clues you need to put the finishing touches on your shooting script and a semi-solid shooting plan. Generally, you need to boil down what is happening in the entire shot into a single picture. This won't look like a finished comic book, but will indicate, without words, exactly what action will occur in that scene. This might indicate a camera pan with arrows or join two scenes together.

They need not be an example of fine art, but it should be apparent to anyone what is supposed to be happening. You may include with these some basic directions, or a general outline of what's happening, but when you're putting them together, it should be obvious (to you at least) what is going on. One trick, when using storyboards to assemble a shooting plan is to cut them into individual frames and to physically put them into order. This can help you get a visual handle on how your shooting is going to proceed, and make you better able to convey that information to your cast.

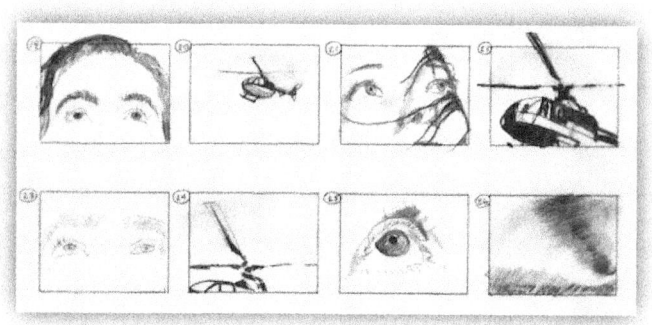

ASSEMBLING THE CAST, CREW AND LOCATIONS

Film is a partnership between yourself, as the director, and your crew. They are certainly there to follow your lead but, also, to give you their time, labor, expertise and suggestions for how to make this a good production they will feel good about seeing their name in credits of. One important aspect of a low-budget shoot is that it should be as short as possible while still allowing enough time to get the coverage you need.

This is especially true if folks are volunteering their time, as a commitment to an entire year of weekends is far harder to make than just two of them. Consider what you'll be asking people to do and you'll get a feel for just how much you can reasonably ask of them.

FINDING COMPETENT PROFESSIONALS TO ASSIST

You'd be surprised how many working professionals are willing to help you put together a trailer for your good idea if they think you can actually sell the idea. For many, helping your movie get sponsorship, by giving their all to make it look good, is akin to a job interview. This is especially true when you are able to assemble a highly skilled and experienced crew. If you're looking to create a film that his both bold and fun, while seeming to have a chance in heck of actually getting funding (for this or another film), you may have access to folks who can guide you into success. When you stack such folks into some key positions, you'll have time to focus on your vision. They are, of course, in demand, so you could loose one or more crew members to higher paying gigs, often right at the last minute (or even in the midst) of your shoot. Be ready to leap in and make a bold change or promotion on the spot. If you trust your intuition and consider the recommendations of other crew members, one can often find at least a suitable stand-in. Ideally, each basic part of the production will have a professional leading their own part of the crew. There certainly can be some overlap – a professional Director of Photography (DP) may be able to use a semi-professional Lighting Director and a small group of amateurs to assist, especially if they've worked together before.

WHEN AMATEURS WILL DO

Maybe it's holding the boom or keeping the shoot free and clear of interference from gawkers. You may not have considered just how many different jobs there are to do in a high-intensity shoot. As long as there is someone to tell your amateurs what to do, it's mostly a matter of getting reliable folks who are genuinely interested in giving up their evenings or weekends to assist. This is true of those "behind the scenes" as well as the actors. Non-speaking roles can be easily handled by your friends and family, as long as they have the right "look." Other jobs can be fairly easily taught with just a few moments of instruction from yourself.

CASTING ACTORS

Though some will swear by it, one of the cardinal rules of being a first-time director is to NOT star in your own film. Sure, make a cameo appearance is fine, but this is not the opportunity to impress anyone with your acting ability. The end result is almost always a less-than-impressive job on both fronts. Choosing actors is partly a matter of getting people who simply look the part and convey in their look the essence of your characters. By the same token, if you're casting a hero, they should look heroic, no matter how good of friends you are. Of course, acting experience is useful. This doesn't have to be film experience, as many theater actors have the chops to follow your direction, even if you do have to subdue their performance a bit. Most importantly, you want someone who won't freeze up when the camera is rolling. Most cities have plenty of actors who are looking to expand their resume, especially if it's a cool project and the finished product will be a piece of video that can be added to their resume. In fact, it is often easier to get actors to volunteer their time than crew members.

LOCATION SCOUTING

Of course, you'll have to make the film somewhere, be that on a set or at an existing location; indoors or out. Even if you plan on starting off with a blue or green-screen trailer, you'll have to put it somewhere. While some folks might recommend running down alleyways, you'll usually want somewhere with reliable electrical outlets, protection from the elements (in the case of a set) and a reasonable noise level. The ideal situation is to find a warehouse or other inexpensive/free location to put a minimal set together. Shooting spaces, when rented as such, are quite expensive. It is not unusual to find that someone on the crew you assemble knows of the very place or the right folks to put you in touch with. Even a building that is still under construction can be a good place, as long as everyone agrees that it's a "no lawsuit" area and that anyone who get wounded has only themselves to blame. Outdoor shoots are often more complicated because of the reliance upon natural lighting, weather and lack of interference from the inherent uncooperativeness of the natural environment. If your shoot is to take place in any sort of inclement environment, such as rain or snow, there will be additional challenges in keeping the equipment from being damaged.

2 - FILM-MAKING STEP BY STEP

Making a film can be a very expensive proposition. Your virginal foray into the craft will need to take advantage of everything possible. Though you will certainly wind up paying for some items, there are several more you can get for free through networking and pitching your idea around to other folks already working in film.

MONEY WELL SPENT

Given a limited budget, you'll have to make some tough decisions about where you'll be speeding your money. If you take a long look at what is most important and your particular circumstances, you may have to re-evaluate what you thought was important.

CAMERA AND SMARTPHONE

Everything begins and ends with a high-quality camera and a good lens package. Often it's best to get a just a few very good lenses, rather than relying upon a large number of mediocre or gimmicky ones. This is very often provided when renting a camera with a basic lens package (Canon EOS 5D Mark II). The look of your film will determine the tone, and if you're looking to make a serious film, your footage should look top notch, and that starts at the lens.

When using a film camera, the quality of the camera itself is not nearly as important as the film itself, but when using digital, the camera is also your film. While a Digital Video (DV) camera and your Smatphone is perfectly good for indoor shoots, you may need to use film or one of the state-of-the-art, very high-resolution digital cameras, such as the Red Digital Camera, when shooting outdoors. Older DV cameras often don't have the dynamic range capable of reproducing high light conditions along with muted lows, as they actually appear in nature, or the ability to compress the visual spectrum as your eye does.

SOUND CAPTURE

There's nothing worse than terrible sound when superimposed on your beautiful film. Most people notice even somewhat poor sound quality well before they are able to discern truly bad lighting. Your job (or that of your "sound department") is to capture as much of the actual sound as possible while eliminating as much of the noise and "bounced" audio. While you can "clean up" a fair bit of the sound in the post-production phase, noise is difficult to clean up and will always be superimposed on the actual dialog. The same is true of voices and noises that bounce off hard surfaces as echo and reverb. Even if you need the room to sound large and empty (as in the case of an abandoned warehouse), in a film, you need the voices to be clear. It's much better to add a bit of digital reverb later than to require removal in post. This can be accomplished by either using a good quality directional microphone or dampening the set and using relatively inexpensive omni-directional microphones. The latter can be done by putting up fabric to cover the hard surfaces in the room you're shooting and positioning your microphone near the actors somehow. For low action scenes, a lavaliere microphone is the device of choice for capturing dialog. This is usually worn clipped on the clothing, out of shot. They are usually *very* small and often wireless. The transmitters can be bulky sometimes, so if doing a long, full-body shot, you may need to make sure to shoot your actors from the front so they can conceal the transmitter behind their backs, usually under the shirt. Wired models are fine for most applications, and often have less noise for a lower cost. Of course, there are plenty of instances where this won't work, such as action or boudoir scenes. For this, a boom is the microphone of choice. This requires a directional microphone as well as an operator with enough upper body strength to keep a relatively heavy mic on a pole up to 14 feet long out of frame in every single shot. If you find the boom is appearing in too many shots, you may need to get someone else to operate it, since this can ruin an otherwise flawless take by the rest of the cast. Try to be as clear as possible about what your frame lines are. You'll often use a mixer to capture sound from several mic sources. A four channel mixer is usually sufficient to capture a sufficient number of sources into a two channel (left and right) mix that can either be superimposed separately onto the video track or fed back into the camera. A digital slate is very often used to give a number for the audio time code as well as the scene, take and reel numbers. Using the right microphones not only saves you time, but can often be procured from your crew members, churches or school radio stations.

MAKE-UP

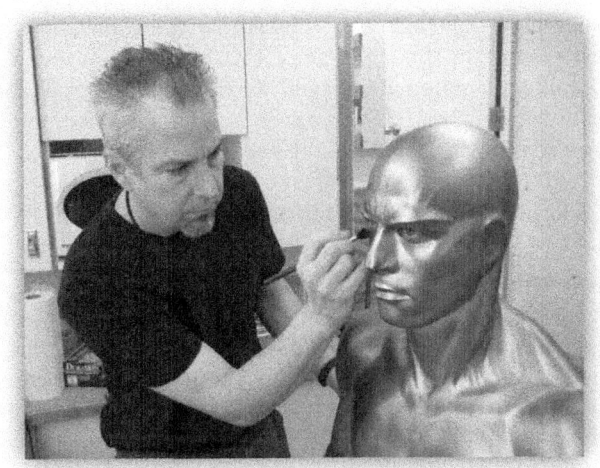

Realistic make up, depending upon your story, can be the difference between an amateurish production and a very convincing appearance. While you may know someone who is very good at hair and make-up, remember that make-up for a film is a very different thing, depending upon whether you need realistic looking blood and guts or just a very steady appearance from one scene to another. If you're lucky, you'll be able to find an experienced make-up artist who will be willing to work on your film for the cost of materials. A good make-up artist will want to take some stills to make sure the make-up is exactly the same from one day of shooting to another, even when a "natural" look is called for. A relatively short shoot that has reasonable hours and good catering will make your shoot a bit more attractive to real professionals. In the case of films that need some extreme make-up elements, look for someone who has not only done this sort of thing before, often in the theater realm. Most professionals will have a portfolio of stills or a short reel of film that you can take a look at when making your decision. It's very much in your best interest to get someone with experience in this role, since this art takes an eye for detail and patience, as well as the ability to reliably show up on time so everyone is ready to go the moment you're ready to begin filming each day.

CATERING AND CRAFT SERVICES

You're responsible for keeping people fed and happy during the shoot. This almost always includes at least one catered meal and a surprising amount of coffee. Since most low-budget shoots will feed their crew on cheap, you can really engender a great deal of goodwill towards your production by providing good quality food. Be advised that good food isn't going to be cheap, but it's always money well spent. This is most especially true if you're getting folks to volunteer their time. You can save some money by making sure you wrap things up before dinner time each day – making it two meals per day and craft services. Such a schedule also means you'll be better able to convince people to give up a weekend day as long as they'll have their nights to themselves. Never underestimate the amount of coffee that a shoot will go through. For a medium-sized shoot with about 30 people to feed every day will go through as much as 2 pounds of coffee per day. It should be fresh and ready to go when your crew shows up in the morning and made all day long, with plenty of cups and add-ins. Be sure you provide plenty of options for your crew members, including vegetarian or kosher options. Though most folks aren't picky, if your vegetarian DP was planning on lunch and all you brought were sausages, you won't get inspired from them in the later afternoon. Most catering professionals are well aware of this and provide plenty of options for everyone.

LIGHTING PACKAGES

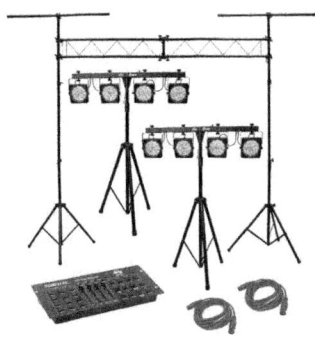

Like any tool, you need the right lights for the job. Sure, you could ask you production crew to fiddle around with cheap lights and try to make it work, but think about what this will do to your production schedule, when you could just get the right equipment in the first place. If you're lucky, your DP will be able to recommend a good lighting crew and grips who can bring lights with them. He or she may have some lights of their own. Take advantage of this. Another option may be asking some film school students to see if they can rent out some gear for their "projects." While it is often advisable to avoid using film school instructors in your shoot, their students can be an invaluable source of inspiration and extra hands that are very willing to leap in and try whatever job you need filled on any given day. Gels are, perhaps, just as important as having lights themselves. This allows you to really take advantage of color in helping to set the tone of your footage. It also allows you to use the same white lights for every scene and to mix and match lights to get the shades you want.

BELIEVABLE SETS

Though you've undoubtedly chosen a script that uses a relatively simple set design, you'll still have to put something together. Even if you're shooting on location, you'll need to manage that location as a set. You may be surprised just how much you can make out of plywood, spray paint, paper and glue. A flat is just a plywood wall you can use to create a wall. They can sometimes be rented from a theatrical supply company, which is much cheaper than buying your own – especially since they usually come with the jack stands that hold them up. If you're renting the flats, you can put up a thin sheet of paper so you can create an entire room or stick a different material up without damaging the flats themselves.

Bear in mind that most sets don't have four walls – two or three is much more common, allowing you to move the camera and lights around. Simple is always best, even if you're creating a whole room. If you know a professional set-dresser, that's great, especially if they're willing to volunteer their services. Otherwise, use some creativity and plan on spending at least one night before the shoot putting the set together. One trick to make you set look more believable; try to keep from the actors a few feet away from the walls if at all possible. This allows you to keep them in sharp focus while using depth of field to let the set blur a bit. Keeping the lighting on the characters soft or from the side is also helpful from keeping hard shadows from falling on those walls.

ITEMS TO WORK AROUND

Elaborate costumes are generally to be avoided. Not only are they expensive to manufacture or procure (unless you have access to a long-time theater company), but you'll also need to maintain them and make sure they're the same between shots. You'll also have to worry about cleaning them, especially if there's some action in your film. It's best to try and get a script that requires as little special clothing as possible.

Dolly tracking is a necessity for moving around a heavy camera in to those smooth tracking shots that really say, "production value." However, you can also break the budget in very short order, even when you rent. One option is to use a skateboard and a dedicated operator. You might be surprised at the quality results you can get, though you must be very careful to make sure the shots are steady, usually necessitating about twice as many takes as you think you'll need. If using film, this could be expensive, so practice takes are in order. You'll also need to make sure the surface you're working on is quite smooth – even a plywood sheet on the floor can show up in camera as shake.

Perhaps one of the most elaborate devices that are commonly used in high-budget films is a Jib arm. They may be many feet long, with 8 feet being a relatively short one. If you do rent one, you'll not only have to spend some time getting used to how to operate it (if your crew doesn't already know), but will also have to make sure you have enough space to accommodate it. That said, this sort of treatment is not generally necessary in most small productions, and it is a testament to your skill at visual storytelling to be able to impress without such gimmicks.

Depending upon where you're planning on filming, you may need to get a whole bevy of permits from the city or county. This can be quite costly, and anything you can do to minimize the number of permits you require, the better off you and your budget will be. There are often private sites that you can use that are as good as or better than public lands. Some semi-private sites that include roads might include colleges during spring break or a loading area for a trucking company. Corporate campuses are often more trouble than they're worth, because of liability issues.

Even as a small production, you may be surprised how many local businesses would be more than happy to trade products and services for a chance to be advertised in your finished product. One especially lucrative sponsorship that can save you a great deal of money is local food and drink companies.

SPONSORSHIP DEALS

For this very reason, you might want to include a scene at a restaurant or even just an opportunity for your characters to be eating or drinking products that are clearly from one of your local proprietors in a shot. Product placement isn't just for big productions – it's a good way to get donations that'll save on the catering/craft services budget.

AVOIDING LEGAL AND LABOR PROBLEMS

One otherwise inconsequential actor can keep your film from ever being finished or released. Avoid this by getting each and every person who will be on camera for even half a second to sign a release form that protects you and your

Incorporation and Limited Liability Corporations (LLC) is a highly recommended option for films that intend to actually make some money or could potentially get someone injured. If your movie is meant to get investors interested and is about two people in a room, having an animated conversation, this isn't really necessary. In the US, each state has its own laws regarding incorporation, and requires at least two (though, usually three or more) people to pony up a small fee, and submit articles of incorporation. That sounds tough, but is really just filling out some forms at the proper state office so you can't be held personally liable if the worst happens. LLC and partnerships are usually the preferred method of handling this, if allowed in your state. They can also be formed in other sates as long as one of the principal signatories resides in that state.

Insurance is a related issue that you'll have to make up your own mind about. Of course, having it means you'll be in a better position to use a wider range of locations, and you'll be entirely "above board." If you've got a funding source, there's no question that part of your budget will include insurance coverage. However, if you're funding the whole project out of your own pocket, you might choose to take a big risk and practice some "guerrilla film-making." But, be advised that this opens you up to a lawsuit if something goes wrong or if someone gets hurt.

USING TONE TO MAKE DIFFICULT SCRIPTS WORK

The maxim among first-time directors is to avoid complicated scripts that involve science-fiction, fantasy, period pieces and anything else that requires elaborate sets, costumes or full-time script supervision. On the other hand, you can make such a script work in certain circumstances by setting the tone of your film.

For instance, a "hard sci-fi" feature film would be folly as a first film, no matter how much you would love it. You may, however, be able to do sci-fi if you do it as an existential comedy. Here, the story and laughs make the effects and realistic portrayal of an entirely different world secondary and forgivable.

In the case of a crime drama, you can "use black as a color" and create a very dark set to obviate the need for complicated sets and expensive location shoots. This sort of "noir" is practical as well as thematic. When you actually get into your production, you'll be able to make a lot of the decisions that will put the finishing touches on the theme you decide to pursue.

3 - PRODUCTION

Here's where you gather all your raw footage. If you don't get it here, as someone on a budget, you just won't have it. Always be ready to get one more shot and try your best to focus your attention on details as well as the wider picture of what your viewing audience will see and experience.

You may be surprised that for all the time you've spent getting a feel for how to compose an elegant shot, what is often most important when it comes time for the actual production is people-management skills.

FILM OR DIGITAL?

Now that some of the high-end digital cameras have begun to shoot with enough resolution to rival the rich, warmth of film, your decision about whether to use a film or digital camera has become tougher. For many it's a simple preference, though there are some truisms to consider.

Film almost always looks better in high-motion outdoor shots. It can bring a warmth that is very hard to approximate with even very good digital cameras. It is also very expensive, especially when you're using new stock that hasn't been sitting in a can for several years. You can't always depend upon development of the film to accurately portray the colors you are looking to capture,

MANAGING PRODUCTION TIME WISELY

Time is money, as they say. Though seemingly trite, nowhere it is more true than during the production of your first film. Since you likely will be on a strict budget, planning out your entire day from the first casting call to the final wrap is vitally important.

Assuming that you've put the leg work in on your pre-production, this will be less of a concern, but problems have a tendency to crop up at the last moment that will require you to make some tough decisions as to scenes that you may have to drop or even changes to the script. Being ready to make such decisions is where your skill as a leader will be required.

STICKING TO A PRODUCTION SCHEDULE

After all the production meetings you've had with your principal crew members, you should have a schedule worked out that details exactly what shots you'll be getting on each day of shooting. For the sake of smooth operations, you *must* stick as closely to this road-map as you possibly can.

That doesn't mean you can't leave time for creativity – this is a creative endeavor, after all. But, the closer you stick to the schedule that outlines the shots you really need, the more likely you are to have some time left over. It's this extra "wiggle" time that you'll work on getting those shots that just came to you during the day's shoot, and often where you get those shots that really can make a stunning visual impact.

THE IMPORTANCE OF PUNCTUALITY

If you're going to expect other people to be on time, you had better be, too. That means getting there before the rest of your crew, along with craft services. If there's one thing people want to see if they've been required to get up at the crack of dawn, it's the person in charge suffering right along with them and a hot cup of coffee, ready to go. Make sure makeup and costuming are also ready before your actors show up.

Films run on a very tight schedule, and your film is no different. A single crew member can hold up a production, causing everyone else to stand around waiting for something to happen. You must have an early enough call time to allow everyone to get settled in and ready before jumping into your aggressive production schedule.

Just as important as starting on time is leaving on time. Of course, you'll be shooting until you get it right, but you really should aim for getting your people home at a reasonable hour, especially if they are due on set first thing the next morning.

KEEPING THE CREW BUSY AND HAPPY

Managing a crew is much like any other type of personal management, in that you will want to make the most of your people while you have them at your disposal. Of course, there is going to be a fair amount of simple standing around, especially by your actors, while each shot is set-up. This can, however, be minimized with careful planning and allowing your lead crewmembers to handle their own departments. For instance, while the lighting crew is setting up a shot, you can engage your actors by rehearsing the next scene with them.

Rehearsal with your actors a few days before the shoot is highly recommended as a good way to make sure that lines and marks run smoothly and according to the production schedule you've hammered out with your production leads. As a general rule, you'll be shooting out of sequence with wide shots moving in to close shots, regardless of how the finished piece will be put together. Getting your actors used to this sequence a few days beforehand will be invaluable for helping you quickly convey what you need when you are on set.

LETTING YOUR CREW MANAGE THINGS

Whether you're dealing with professionals or others who are doing it for the first time, you need to trust your crew to do their jobs, so you can do yours. That doesn't mean ignoring what others are doing, as you will still need to keep an eye out for mistakes and instances were mistakes are likely to take place, but it does mean that you can't allow yourself to become preoccupied with minutia.

Film is a collaborative effort, and you need to make sure your crew knows they can give you their advice at any time. As a first-time director, you need to make sure that you listen to all their ideas, take them into consideration and make a decision. Sometimes this will be done on the fly. You certainly don't have to explain yourself if you don't take a crew-member's idea, but there should be no doubt that you are the person in charge of making the decisions. This is your baby, after all.

DIRECTOR OF HOTOGRAPHY / CINEMATOGRAPHER

Directing a film doesn't mean you'll need to have your finger on every single button. A director of photography (DP) is an invaluable resource who actually gets the shots so you can concentrate on making decisions about them.

In very small productions, the director can also take on DP duties, though things usually run more smoothly the more of these you can hand off. If this is your first time directing, you'll need to rely upon the advice of an experienced DP, so getting the very best person you can for this role is the most important slot to fill, from an artistic standpoint.

Of course, a film is about more than art. That's where your assistants and producers come in.

FIRST ASSISTANT DIRECTOR

Catering to your needs and keeping you on the set so there isn't any down time, the First Assistant Director (AD). Some folks liken them to cattle herders. This is one of the most important jobs on the set, and the organizational skills of your First AD are extremely important. Though often viewed as a "gatekeeper" for the director, they are primarily responsible for translating the creative whims of the director into specific direction for the other principal crew-members.

Usually endowed with a booming voice, the First AD is also responsible for calling for action, announcing a "ready" state for the crew and, when the sound and second cameras should be ready to roll in anticipation of primary camera engagement.

Some other common duties of a First AD might include:

- Announcing which department the production is waiting on
- Calling for quiet on the set
- Clearing the production area of bystanders and non-essential personal
- Making sure the production is progressing according to the shooting schedule
- Directing extras and scene changes
- Scouting for locations
- Coordinating the activities of the Line Producer

LINE PRODUCER / PRODUCTION COORDINATOR

Sometimes not even found on the set, line producers are the office managers of your film. This role is often co-mingled with that of the first AD on small shoots, but either way, someone is going to have to make copies and handle the paperwork. Additionally, small-budget features may wrap some of the functions of wardrobe and makeup

Think of them as someone who is the First AD for the production itself rather than the director her or himself. Some of the many tasks assigned to the Line Producer/Production Coordinator might include:

- Making sure there are enough copies of the script for everyone
- Helping create and manage the budget
- Locating and hiring ancillary crew members
- Manage catering and craft services
- Making sure there's suitable parking for everyone
- Wrangling wardrobe at the last minute
- Handling permits and legal matters
- Going on emergency supply runs
- Disseminating and filing all the personal and location release forms
- Phone calls
- Gopher runs for last-minute supplies
- Photocopying "call sheets" and "production reports"
- Making sure all the equipment is returned on time and in good condition

SCRIPT SUPERVISOR

The odds are very good you'll be shooting out of sequence. Someone will have to pay attention to exactly where your characters are in the script, and that's what a script supervisor does. You'll be spending so much time making sure the delivered dialog and images are just so; you won't have time to constantly be consulting your script. In terms of continuity, the first day is the only one you can get by without one.

This duty is often closely related to that of a "Clapper Loader" on a larger shoot, making sure the slates match for each scene in the audio and video. If this aspect of the film is screwed up, the editing process is damned to extra hours of searching for the right footage and making it difficult to put everything together during the rough edit.

YOUR ROLE AS DIRECTOR

You are, in short, the decision maker. This is your vision, and it's your job to make sure that what you imagine is actually what's being shot. You will function as the final word, and since there's so much going on, it's hard to rise above all the confusion and focus upon nothing beyond what's required artistically. Since you will likely be getting much of your labor for low or no prices, it's also your job to be genial to everyone who is reporting to you in one way or another.

It is definitely your role to always be on the set, if possible. If something needs to be done off-set, let one of your assistants handle it for you and report back. If you don't have an assistant, you need to put off what you can and quickly deal with what you must to maximize your time on set. You will be making the final decision about everything, and your crew can't proceed without your input and okay of lighting and shooting decisions.

Some other tasks might include:

- Calling for lunch and breaks
- Making minimal script changes
- Interfacing with your first AD
- Calling for "cut" at the end of each scene

DIRECTING ACTORS

As the director, you'll be spending much of your time between takes getting everything you can from your acting talent. There are innumerable books on the topic. One of the most often cited is Judith Weston's influential and well-respected book <u>Directing Actors</u>, which is a very in-depth text on this art and craft. Generally, you'll be telling your actors not so much what they'll be feeling as much as explaining the characters to them, giving them character background and allowing them to bring their own emotional interpretation to the role.

Often times if their feet are out of frame, you can simply mark the floor with a piece of tape. Otherwise, in the case of long shots, you'll just have to practice it and make sure things look right in the monitor. This may involve a few more takes, but it's better than catching a piece of tape in frame.

Rehearsals with your actors are usually done dry a few days before the shoot and quickly on camera on the day of the shoot before the film is actually rolling. The actors must know exactly where they're to stand, where their hands and heads are for each and every scene.

It's generally a good idea to focus your attention on your monitor or through a viewfinder, since looking back and forth between the reality and the captured footage can be confusing.

GETTING THE COVERAGE YOU NEED

The old adage in production is that you'll take twice as many shots of any given scene that you think you'll need and then one more. While this may sound excessive, there are so many variables at work in even the simplest shoot, that you'll need every single one of those takes to really get what you're looking for.

At the minimum, you'll be taking at least 3 shots of everything before moving on to the next scene. Don't be afraid to keep doing it until it seems right. It is not entirely uncommon, for instance, to do upwards of 20 takes of a very complicated scene. You're not an ogre for making everyone do it over and over again – you're simply getting it right.

Be especially careful to keep an eye out for unfortunate reflections, rogue tire tracks, continuity mistakes and other small details that will become glaring problems in the editing process. If working with a scene that is likely to be troublesome, give yourself the advantage by getting a few extra takes for good luck.

MONITORING TAKES

If using the talents of a DP, you'll be spending most of the actual shoot time behind a remote monitor. It is rare that you'll actually need to look through the camera's viewfinder or internal monitor, though it is often a good idea to check and make sure that what you're seeing in the monitor jibes with what your DP is seeing.

When using film, you'll be back with the camera using a viewfinder. These are small viewfinders that allow you to adjust for the exact aspect ratio you'll be shooting in. There are different standards for television, film and panorama (letter-boxed) presentation. You'll have to decide which you'll use before you begin filming.

A used viewfinder can be obtained for as little as a hundred dollars and is useful regardless of the medium employed, though essential for film. In a pinch, you can use a piece of cardboard cut out to the specific ratio you're using or even your hands. Most experienced DPs will have their own.

WHEN TO CALL IT A WRAP

Since you've seen this film in your head from the time you picked out your script, you have to trust that you'll instinctively know when to call it a wrap. Though you may get advice from the other members of your crew, often along with suggestions for changing some little thing to help you get that take just right, the ultimate judgment is yours.

Your shoot schedule is also a determining factor. You will have already gotten all the shots you absolutely *need*, but what is perhaps a bit more difficult to get a handle upon is when to decide that you've gotten a reasonable number of shots that you *want*. When you look at your script and suddenly realize that you've covered everything, it's a wrap.

Be sure and tell everybody what a wonderful job they've done and how very much you appreciate it. Give them a rough time frame for when you'll all get together and view the finished product. If there's anything a cast and crew love as much as the film itself, it's the wrap party. This has the added advantage of allowing you to let your cast know how much you appreciate their effort and give everyone a copy of the finished product for them to show their friends.

If you've had production stills taken, be sure and get them copies of those as soon as possible. The web makes it easy to disseminate such information, giving your crew something to show others while they're waiting for you to put the finished product together in post.

4 - POST-PRODUCTION

The post-production is where you'll be bringing your vision to life. You'll be using this process to take those disparate shots and assemble them into a coherent whole. This is also the process by which you'll assemble production stills and choose the best shot from a large number of takes. This process can take many times longer than the actual shoot, but is also a much less collaborative process, where you can gather all the production elements together into something viewable.

Since you're likely doing this with a small budget, you probably won't be able to do "pick-up" shots in case every shot of a given scene has been fouled up somehow. This means that you may have to cut out some shots that you really thought you needed. This is easier to do in the case of a trailer rather than a short film. One way around this is to crop in on a shot, as is often done when the boom is in frame – as long as you're not just cutting the top of your character's head off, this can sometimes be even more effective than what you had planned. Be prepared to be flexible in the edit bay.

VIDEO

First and foremost, as an inherently visual medium, you'll be looking to put together a good looking film. Whether using film or digital, you'll be splicing and dicing together a story during this process. Special effects are usually added towards the end of the editing process, sometimes after the final edit, but usually after the rough cut.

Generally, the process involves creating a rough cut that you'll use as your guide to assemble a final cut. You'll be taking notes from the raw footage as to what takes seem like the best ones, and then making a "scratch" copy that you can make further notes as to exactly where you'll be making the cuts and splices on the real film. The latter process is usually the least time consuming, but don't under estimate how long it will take you to go through all the footage you took. A five minute trailer, for instance, can take you and an editor as much as five long days to fully wrangle into a finished product.

USING YOUR HOME COMPUTER OR A GOOD POST HOUSE

In a "post-house," you and a technician will be sitting together in a room with a state-of-the-art computer, virtually chopping up and splicing the "down-rezed" scratch-footage as well as your final, high-resolution footage that will be delivered directly to CD or for distribution as final reels.

As a director, you'll ideally work with an editor who wasn't actually at the shoot. Aside from the experience of a trained editor, this is important because, as a director, you've got too much time and love invested in this project to be able to mercilessly cut scenes that don't actually further the story, no matter how beautiful they may be. When particularly nice footage is discarded for story reasons, the unsavory term, "baby killing," is used to convey the angst some directors feel when confronted with such a choice. A dedicated editor is, in a sense, your first test audience.

One of the other advantages of a good post house is that they will have copies of very expensive and necessary film editing software. Avid and Final Cut Pro are the two most commonly used programs. Though it is certainly not unheard of for a very small-budget film to be cobbled together on software that was borrowed from a friend, this can get you into big legal trouble should you unexpectedly have a minor hit on your hands.

One way around this is to barter for the services of someone who runs their own freelance post-house during the day. By doing the work in non-peak hours and times, often accepting that you can be pushed out of the way for real, paying work, you can often get access to real equipment and editing talent for a fraction of the cost. This is especially true of interesting projects in markets where people make their bread and butter putting together corporate training videos and other drudgery.

You can save their time by taking some time before you go in and trashing the cuts that are clearly not suitable. This is very often done when you try to create in-camera effects that require many, many takes. You'll want to trash the clearly unsuitable takes so you can use your edit time as efficiently as possible.

FINAL EDIT

If using a typical DV camera, you can do the final edit on a copy (always make a back up ideally with a

RAID configured storage device – your footage is precious!) of the raw footage, though if using a home-model Mac or PC, you might need to take it down to "standard resolution" to do editing on your less powerful machine.

Of your "off line" or low-resolution print that you'll be making your practice edit with, you'll have a script with notes as well as software marks. It's usually fairly quick work to use a very fast computer to take that "on-line" or full-resolution edit and make a copy that's ready to be output into standard DVD format, with menus and everything.

It is not unusual to do the rough cut work on a home computer and then use an edit house for the final work. It's up to you and very dependent upon your budget, since they usually charge by the hour.

COLOR CORRECTION

No matter how good your lighting, you'll be doing some color correction to make up for variables that inevitably during shooting. This can be done for the same physical location that has been shot at two different times even just to punch up contrast or specific colors.

Color correction is done with a computer program when using a digital camera. When using film this is usually transferred to video for the process and then a new negative is cut. This is applied to an entire film using a bypass filter that gives a "look" to the entire edited product or individual scenes as a "color-style," such as the bleach-bypass that is sometimes done to make film look old.

AUDIO

Even a very well recorded production will need to have some work done to the audio, including adding music, sound effects and sometimes actually re-recording dialog. You can even use a different voice actor to lip-sync or even run dialog through a digital filter to change the pitch or timbre. Again, while much of this can be done in a home recording studio, it's always valuable to elicit the help of a professional that has done this for some time and is willing to trade or donate services for the chance at a credit and a potential gig working on your next production that actually pays.

ADDITIONAL DIALOG RECORDING (ADR)

No matter how good your actors or sound techs are, you'll almost certainly have to do a bit of pick up on the other end. This will be done in a recording studio, usually with your actors. Doing as little of this as possible is certainly the goal, but it's hard to avoid. Don't be afraid to change the audio if it just isn't right. You'll know if the sound and images don't seem to match.

Another common use of ADR is to add dialog where you've been required to make cuts in the footage or where your actors have messed up their lines in an otherwise good take. This is done with superimposing a very noiseless take of the actors' voice on top of a loop of "room tone," or about 30 seconds of quiet that is usually recorded before each scene as a base line. Your sound engineer will endeavor to re-create as closely as possible the sound and type of mic that was used in that take, too.

Voice overs are also a common use of ADR, especially in the case of trailers. Though you'll not likely use a professional voice-actor to do such work, you will usually use the standard booming voice that gets peoples' attention.

FOLEY

The time-honored art of sound effects is more commonly known in the industry as Foley, and there are plenty of plenty of opportunities of it in even the simplest shoots. This includes the sound of feet, fight sounds, gunfire or any ambient noise that you're hoping to include to set the tone of the scene, such as truck traffic outside a diner.

This also includes creating the sound of a room, even if that's not the sort of room you're using. For instance, if you're filming a scene that's supposed to be in a metal vault, but your set is a thin sheet of metal over plywood, you'll need to actually make the room sound "metallic" by adding an effected track as a "layer."

OUTPUT AND DISTRIBUTION

Once you're finally and reasonably satisfied with what you've got, the first thing you want to do is to show what you've got to someone who knows nothing about your film to see if it makes sense. If they don't get it, you may have to go back and re-cut it. If they like it, it's time to make copies.

Your final high-file will be taken to a "mastering house" to bulk duplicate the DVD for you. Often you can make your own labels and design the packaging. This can be done very convincingly by just about anyone with a good design sense and graphic manipulation software such as Photo Shop.

Now that you've got a finished product, you need to get it to either the movie theaters you want to show or to the folks with money that you want to impress. Don't underestimate the amount of time you'll need to invest to actually get folks to see your film – you've just entered the realm of marketing.

Whether done for profit or love, this is the part of the production where everyone is relying upon you to make something happen. This is where most businesses that fail don't do their homework. This is, by no coincidence, exactly what most artists dread. Networking, in person, online or by phone is the best way to really make the sort of connections that you'll need to use in an effort to meet the people that can actually make things happen for you.

Distribution is a major topic and endeavor in its own right, but some new options have opened up in recent years for those looking to make money, such as the direct-to-DVD overseas market and direct online distribution though your own website or through a service such as i Tunes or even through the film distribution networks of major hotels or airlines.

If you're making a short film or a trailer, you can upload this to You Tube or other online video sites such as atom films or I-films. You can't expect people to pay to see a short film unless it's part of a touring short film showcase that plays in theaters. You can also enter festivals, allowing people to give your project some recognition and, hopefully, create something of a buzz among monied interests looking to invest. A short film is your calling card to bigger and better things.

CONCLUSION

You really can make a film. It's a process like any other, but one that certainly relies upon the talents and experience of many people. If you've got a really good idea and a vision, it will be infectious and creative people will want to help you be a success.

Remember, it never hurts to ask. Keep asking, and something amazing just might happen.

Good Luck!